Keith

Out of the Weather

Julie Mellor

What a pleasure to be able to sign this for you. I love your poems!

Julie

smith|doorstop

Published 2017 by
smith|doorstop books
The Poetry Business
Bank Street Arts
32-40 Bank Street
Sheffield S1 2DS

ISBN 978-1-912196-00-5
Typeset by Utter
Printed by Biddles

Acknowledgements
Versions of some of these poems were previously published in *Ambit, Brittle Star, Butcher's Dog, The Frogmore Papers, Mslexia, The North, The Rialto, The Interpreter's House, Spokes* (Otley Word Feast Press) and *Stand.* Some of the poems have also been placed in the following open poetry competitions: Barnet, Havant, Ilkley and Nottingham. Thanks are also due to the Voices in the Landscape project at Wentworth Castle, Stainborough, where 'Harriet in the Glasshouse' first appeared.

smith|doorstop books are a member of Inpress:
www.inpressbooks.co.uk. Distributed by Central Books Ltd.,
99 Wallis Road, London E9 5LN

The Poetry Business gratefully acknowledges the support
of Arts Council England.

Contents

They could lay bare in the utmost detail everything that you had done or said or thought; but the inner heart, whose workings were mysterious even to yourself, remained impregnable.

George Orwell, *1984*,
Penguin, 2003 (f.pub. Martin Secker and Warburg Ltd., 1949)

The Scar on my Wrist

Yellow stars of skin where the break was pinned,
a car crash, Hereford, student weekend
of Pernod and black, my friends,

Susan with the cowlick fringe,
her boyfriend from the Rhonda,
and Steve, who would run naked down any street

at midnight for a dare, all of us in a hire car,
speeding down that road with the hidden bend,
scream of wheels spinning mid air,

the roof crushed in the long roll down the bank
and us, after our minute's silence,
clambering out with no more than a graze,

except for the compound fracture to my wrist,
and weren't we the lucky ones, in love
with ourselves, the resilience of our bodies

taken for granted, and didn't we drink ourselves
stupid the following night, quoting Talking Heads,
this ain't no party, this ain't no disco,

this ain't no fooling around, me with my arm in plaster,
flirting with the fireball from a box of matches,
a pub trick that set my face alight.

Darling, What if…

What if I choose this one small fly, iridescent on the daisy's white ruff.

What if I choose to follow it with my eye from flower to flower
as I sit on this bench, a wooden sleeper resting on two grindstones.
And what if other flies circle, for example, that fat atheist the bluebottle,
searching for something more akin to a shopping mall than a lawn.

What if nothing happens but sound, trains across the way
sliding in and out of town like pharmaceutical salesmen or lovers
who've met on the internet. What if the wind repeats rumours
of their wedding vows from mid-week town hall ceremonies.

What if the fly disappears, only for a minute, but completely,
dizzying blindly through a portal into another world.

I know this can't happen, because a fly has a thousand eyes
and can't go anywhere blindly. Imagine our world as it appears to the fly,
like a shop front on a 70s high street, stacked with tvs,
all tuned to the same channel.

This is the closest you'll ever get to understanding, not being a fly,
but at least being able to picture it, the feeling inside my messed-up head.

The Lodging House

after L.S. Lowry

The lamp burns above the doorway
grey as a pearl   faces queue

without bodies   men whose lungs
are clogged with cotton dust

hands in empty pockets
tongues   without words

this is the time of day
when pigeons attempt to coo

where the breath moves
like a child among overcoats

and net curtains shift   against
the casual undressings of the heart.

Penitential

Walking barefoot to Paradise Square,
I pass the gym where Japanese students
work their bodies to perfection.

There is no weather, just heat.
I head for the subway to relive old times;
going home from a gig with nothing

on my mind except music,
feel the weight of closed shops,
the concrete walls scrawled with graffiti,

the cheap hotel that promises SLEEP.
A drunk holds out his arms as if to embrace me,
but I know I have to get to Paradise Square,

to kneel before the brand new Audis
parked on double yellow lines,
to look up at those Regency windows

where solicitors in white silk shirts
are working late and receive
the blessing of their immaculate advice.

Propolis

I'm aware it's the stuff of bee spit and wax,
that it turns soft when the sun warms the hive,

and the bees, busy with their work of sealing the gaps,
are animate and fondling in their movement.

In truth, it's not propolis I'm talking about,
but those unwanted spaces where words land and rest.

Think of old windows, how the putty has hardened
under layers of paint so the glass rattles loose in the frame.

When I say it's turning cold, remind you
to shut the door to stop the draught,

what I'm really saying is, here is my heart,
raw as lambs' liver, leaking on a white plate.

It shouldn't be so exposed. There shouldn't be
all this stale air around it.

Dear Heron

When I saw you in that glass case with the handy leather strap so you could be carried about like luggage, I noticed you were a bird of two addresses: ID No. 56, Shelf K, being your indoor place and Acres Hill, just north of here, where they shot you through the heart (which I imagine to be shrivelled, like Shelley's – although after forensic examination that turned out to be his liver).

Heron, you're as common as newspaper. Your neck has all the elasticity of one of those foam floats shaped like draught excluders that children use when they're learning to swim. I have memories of you struggling to take off from the river Don and how you were so nervous I could never get close.

I don't hold it against you. When I look at you now, all the ungainliness of flight gone, I think the dry and hollow body, the wire frame instead of bones, is all any of us has.

Architecture

I stoop under the Gothic arch,
my face pale as Cadeby's limestone,
a broken layer that outcrops here at Roche,

the fun fair parked off Bawtry Road
colouring the air with diesel fumes
and the smell of spun sugar.

Some nights, water drips like tears
through my seams and fractures,
wasps in my masonry papering themselves in

for another long winter.
A torch will give you all the facts,
how the curls in my hair crumble to dust

and love has become a word so underused
it settles on my chest like the weight of books.
Take what you want,

lead, pewter, the hoard of coins
buried beyond the perimeter.
Bones in their unmarked graves

give themselves up after months of rain.
Laughton Pond overruns.
The paths become muddy, impassable.

Kids come here to shelter, scrawl their names:
carved initials, the graffiti of hearts.
Remember what lasts, what fades.

Study of the Structures of Flight

after a photograph by Dorit Hockman

What are we
so soft we are mortified
shall we ever be born
fledging under glass
foetal nubs
when is our colour coming
why are we cauled
growing shy in the sense
we send out
on the rebound
nothing comes back
blinding our ears
why do we ripen
late as pears
why are we having
to eke out our skin
why are our wings
unable to stretch
dissected with light
what if we die
is sleep a long time
will the air feed us
is it true the moon.

Sometimes I Think of the Edwardians

The way they fell in love with electricity,
how they went so wild for it they tried to run
their lives off a single socket,
plugged in curling tongs and standard lamps,
because electricity didn't smell like they were used to with gas,
then someone invented the steam iron
and the circuit overloaded and the house burnt down.

I once saw the way electricity travels
illustrated by wire wool connected to a car battery,
a small universe, full of surges and collisions,
energy moving over itself until something failed
and started to smoke, which made me think
of Edison who, for safety's sake,
put the fuse into mass production,
by which time the craze had turned to Radium
and women went all out for steel-ribbed corsets
painted with it, broke their own ribs
so their tiny waists would glow in the dark.

Out of the Weather

Higher than hail or snow,
we watch it in other people's lives,
cars on the Woodhead Pass,
stranded beetles in rush hour,
red lights at Holme Moss and Emley Moor
warning through low cloud,

higher than this, looking down
on the small world of the bowling club,
men in tee shirts, pints in hand, in the rain,
in a match won by the one
who doesn't retreat to the bar.

We watch them, bleached by floodlights,
a shine that's twice a full moon
and ten times as spiritual, and we pray for them,
out in their weather, as we pray for those
who dash with trolleys across Tesco's
miraculous car park, shimmering, soaked.

Clog Field

The view is Sheffield's skyline, sun on slate,
weather changing from poor to fair,

heat through trees and flies hatching,
stone-clad houses, back-yard extensions,

allotments with their umpteen front doors,
the haze of privet and Clog Field

pulling against my boot soles,
its name unknown beyond Bannerdale

and Carterknowle, this small acre
where the city's horses used to graze,

the only place to rest a lame one
or give a mare space to drop her foal,

here, on the edge of Brincliffe Woods,
the field's boundary an outcrop of stone.

To Say We Exist

after Stephen Dobyns

How profound to be a miner,
ascending in a steel cage,
that end of shift fatigue momentarily lifted
only to be shouldered again the following day.

Think also of the diver, swimming towards
the thinning colour that is surface;
how dangerous that epiphany
when nitrogen enters the bloodstream.

This feeling has been with me
since childhood, when I stayed in a strange bed
troubled by the ornaments of other people's lives,
the shape of the dressing gown

hung behind the door, listening
to the constant passage of trains in the night,
coal trucks I lay awake and counted,
or counted because I lay awake.

The Army Medical Corps Handbook

The suffocated dark
of the book's small print
          filled with expertise
where the blood flowed   from the days when
those lines and destinations
                    mapped the body

a handbook of circuits
blue and red   the patient partially I
a stand in   trying to read
this little diagram   one page
of how we are

the heart is attendant
knows how to stem any emergency
things are dealt with   stitched
we were   we are   think of that
a map like the underground   empty platforms
ghost stations

misted glass and your name
your name speeding past.

Wasps

Out of kilter with the season,
they cruise the warmth from the security light
on the oak beam inside the barn.

Lime-washed walls, cobwebs slung
like small hammocks to nurse them
through lengthening nights.

The air's turning damp;
one hard frost might claim them.
But they blaze against death,

bodies brittle as sweet wrappers,
the inked nibs of their stings
constantly primed.

From the bulb's discarded heat
they lower themselves to cooler air
like drops of oil through water,

a move I don't fully understand.
Sometimes they disappear into gaps
between wall and lintel,

or cling to the rafters, guarding
their paper monasteries, filling
my head with memories,

seven years old under the plum tree's
swarming branches, dropped fruit
fermenting on the lawn,

the sudden burn of drunken fury
from the one I brushed away,
the half-smoked cigarette, years later,

stubbed out on my inner arm,
the same inarticulate pain.

The Honey Baron

i

The Honey Baron carries a jar of light in his pocket. He says, *Look at this and tell me you don't understand.* He offers it as a cure for hay fever and says it was used to heal wounds on the battlefield at the time of the Iceni. The Honey Baron is a man who knows his history. He boasts, *This jar bears my name and the substance it holds can withstand time. Open it 100 years from now and it will have lost none of its potency.* He pronounces *potency* in a very solemn voice, like a man who wishes to be buried with his horse.

ii

The Honey Baron says gleefully, *You'll be like lobsters tomorrow,* which means he's going to take the lid off his jar of light, and allow us to bask in its vinegary glow until our skin burns, which means he'd like to see us peel, right down to our curtain rails, our coat hangers, right down to our umbrella frames, our laths and struts, our tent poles, our chicken wire, our garden fences, our food processors, our safety chains, our under-wired, lemon satin, lace-trimmed, 34B, balconette style bras, made in Italy with matching knickers.

iii

At dusk, the Honey Baron screws the lid on tight. The sky folds itself into a little square, 7 folds exactly and no more, because it's impossible to fold anything in half more than 7 times. The Honey Baron has tried and even with the tissue paper from his wife's Seville oranges, it can't be done. He pushes the jar back into his waistcoat pocket where it warms itself against his gall stones. In his newly mown field, visitors are unwinding orange extension leads and hooking up to his electricity supply. They switch on their low voltage appliances and bask in the hum of night lights.

Aftermath

On the way back I was cool as glass,
damp cool the way condensation settles
on the windscreen, early morning,
late October. I was hard as glass too,

hard the way a marble is hard
until rolled against a steel bearing
and realises it's cracked. I was mulling
it over. You were up there

on the surface of the moon and I
was hurtling towards the earth,
like that man testing the limit
of the human body by rising, high altitude

in a helium balloon, then jumping
back to earth at 700 mph, hoping
that when he exceeded the speed of sound
he would simply feel the air ripple

over his streamlined body, feel like an eel
swimming upriver in spring, not start
to break up, lose consciousness,
not feel anymore.

Divining

On bad nights I think of Jim Longton,
somewhere out in the stubble,
trousers tucked into the tops of his boots,
arms bent as if to steady a horse or fire a gun,
pointing instead the length of brass he communes with.

On bad nights I want to be party
to what passes between him and the metal,
the questions which sound rhetorical,
though the rod answers with the conviction
of a weather vane

and he follows, mapping the fields
to prove this dried-out land was once tidal,
divining the place where King John's baggage train
sank in the salt-marsh,
the drowning of men and royal regalia.

On bad nights, I want him
to show me the future, though river and sea
clash on an in-breath and whatever shortcut
the land seems to offer
disappears under the weight of water.

Grace Notes

I see you walking across the marsh,
blue shirt and khaki shorts,
flat land and flat sky meeting behind you,

ripples of water through coarse grass
etching the danger you're treading.
Quicksand. Tides.

I need to call you back
to the curved wall of the promenade
where salt grass has been flattened

by the storm surge. I want you
to stand here, looking out over the bay
where Heysham Power Station rises

like a bleak temple, to hear the flight
of black swans pass overhead, grace notes
drifting from the hinges of their wings.

Here

Where the road stops at the rim of the world,
past the house where my grandmother
cooked for twenty years on a Primus stove

at the top of the cellar steps, the road
where my father won the slow bike race
in 1953, where our uncles had biblical names,

Nicodemus, Diadorous, and our aunt was unrelated,
an evacuee who never went home, where family
is still family, though most are long gone.

Sunday Afternoons

I'm sad when I think about money
in the same way I'm sad when I think about Byzantine mosaics,
or frescoes ruined by damp, the misplaced fidelity
of gold leaf as it clings to flaking plaster.

I'm sad when I look at people in museum cafés
who sit alone, how they invariably wear blue,
like photographs of people at the seaside in rain.

I'm sad for the Victorian schoolgirl in love with Ruskin,
who painted *The Biography of a Snowdrop*.

I'm sad when my phone rings and I'm sad when it doesn't.

I'm sad when a stretch limo cruises past
and I remember the yellow silk jacket I tried on
in Topshop on Tottenham Court Road in 1985.

I'm sad for creatures like tortoises and hedgehogs
that sleep through the reckless beauty of winter.

I'm sad for peacock feathers in vases and 1930s cocktail hats,
although occasionally my spirits lift, as they do
when I stand in front of the hand-coloured aquatint
of turtle doves, drawn by John James Audubon
against a background of white-flowered Stuartia.

February

I went with the weather,
the white bones of steady rain,

the idea of rain in woodlands
where birch trees are leased in spring
to give their sugary sap.

I thought of the body, how it bleeds,
how cut rain moves,
how leaves shiver.

If I could choose to be just one thing
it would be a tree

and that tree would be birch
for the first cut of spring,
for the beautiful wound,

to fall in with the lengthening of days.

One of These Days

We'll clear out the cupboard under the stairs,
where a bag of sticks is slumped, netted in orange nylon
like a catch of shellfish, and coal for tonight's fire
stands next to the bucket of ash from every morning this week.

We'll clear out old coats that hang,
with the smell of dogs, behind the latched door,
the tins of paint with skins thick as rice pudding
cooked in the oven-bottom.

We'll clear out firelighters, so damp they've melted
like soap left too long at the side of the bath,
and torches whose bulbs have yellowed to cast nothing
into this great dark.

We'll sweep the slate floor of footprints
and burn the pile of newspapers stacked to the roof
like a pillar of salt in a Cheshire mine, where Victorian visitors
would marvel at the size of the cavern, those hewn pillars

holding up a roof the size of a football pitch,
a hole fifteen feet above their heads to let down a rope
and a glimpse of sky, and I wonder if that dayhole held true,
like the Pantheon's roof, against the insistent rain.

Partial Eclipse

I want to exchange the weather
for something kinder. Clouds break.
Hail falls like tiny bones.

These are the days I walk through,
tending small ambitions,
the low comedy of us at home.

Sometimes I worry our charm
is stinted. If I tell you pins
lie under my tongue, there so long

I've sucked on the tang of iron
and thought it was blood.
We stand in the garden, looking

through dark glass. Air turns to winter,
morning evades us. The moon
is awkward across the face of the sun.

Harriet in the Glasshouse

This morning I walked under glass and felt my body lighten.
Small bursts of applause from the rain,

my breath lifted with the warm updraft of marvellous engineering,
iron grates cut in the shape of passionflowers.

This morning I learnt about my voice, how when it comes up
against a rippled pane it vanishes.

I learnt that men hunt down unusual seeds like they hunt wild animals,
that they are prepared to risk their lives to attach their name to a flower.

I listened to the panic of the trapped fly that was unable to comprehend
the true meaning of its captivity.

I read about the seeds of shrubbier plants which only germinate when exposed
to smoke, and thought of those other great invigorators: fire, ice.

When the sky finally made itself known, I looked up to it
as I look up to my father, admiring all his certainties,

felt the sun in the names of his early African introductions: Pelargonium,
Gladioli, yearned for that American luxury, the pineapple.

Life: A User's Manual

Like an apartment block with the front removed,
Perec's novel of a thousand intertwined lives
and addresses, the logic of who lives on the first floor
at number 20, who lived there before
and how that's relevant to the family on the third floor
who emigrated, but not before they'd buried
the husband's younger brother, the one with a flaw
so deep it surfaced in their dreams.

The dreams themselves are on another storey,
where the concierge uses the master key to let himself in
using the mathematics of the number 3,
a magic number, relevant to everything we do,
so our lives are in this book too, like the man
who makes it his business to track down the au-pair
who drowned his only child in the bath
using a series of calculations based on the probability
that any closing chapter ends in a rented room,
the television talking quietly to itself,
a couple asleep on their backs.